William Hall

The victory of defeat and other poems

Chiefly on hebrew themes

William Hall

The victory of defeat and other poems
Chiefly on hebrew themes

ISBN/EAN: 9783744722759

Printed in Europe, USA, Canada, Australia, Japan

Cover: Foto ©Lupo / pixelio.de

More available books at **www.hansebooks.com**

The Victory of Defeat

And Other Poems.

VICTORY OF DEFEAT,

AND OTHER POEMS,

Chiefly on Hebrew Themes.

BY

WILLIAM HALL, M.A.

LONDON:
SWAN, SONNENSCHEIN & CO., Ltd
1896.

[ALL RIGHTS RESERVED.]

PRINTED BY
LANG NEIL, LONDON AND BRIGHTON.

CONTENTS.

	PAGE.
THE VICTORY OF DEFEAT	1
SUSPIRIA	41
THE CORRECTED ESTIMATE	49
THE QUIETED SOUL	61
THE PURPOSE OF THE AGES	67
THE ETERNAL REFUGE	91
BEFORE THE BATTLE	103
TRANSFIGURATION THROUGH SUFFERING	113
THE REDEEMED CITY	121
THE DISCIPLINE OF PAIN	153
IN EXITU ISRAEL	165
A PEOPLE FOR HIS PRAISE	175
EPICTETUS	183

THE VICTORY OF DEFEAT.

THE VICTORY OF DEFEAT.

I.

In the great conflict hour of human life
    That cometh, without fail, to one and all,
When the supernal powers are at strife,
    Wrapt is the spirit in sepulchral pall.

Hedged is our path as with sharp, thick-set thorns,
    Walled up the way that we were wont to tread;
Removed far from us all that life adorns,
    Lover, friend, kinsman, and acquaintance fled.

THE VICTORY OF DEFEAT.

On mourra seul; the soul's decease alike
  Evades the vulgar gaze, the general eye :—
Into gross earth unseen it erst did strike,
  Viewless it enters on its stage next high.

Beneath a canopy of murky dark—
  So dense the hurtling bolts throng the dun air—
Speeds the fell fight—illumined by no spark,
  Beam from faint tremulous star, or moonlight
    fair ;—

So thick the hellish hosts that issue forth
  From the black womb of the abysmal night ; —
Thus her cloud-armies pours the cold bleak north,
  The tender hopes of budding spring to blight.

Valley of shadowing death ! arena grand !
  There our great crowning victories are won ;
Surrendering guilty self a deodand—
  We feel the true, the eternal life begun.

AND Jacob was left alone; and there wrestled a man with him until the breaking of the day. And when he saw that he prevailed not against him, he touched the hollow of his thigh, and the hollow of Jacob's thigh was out of joint, as he wrestled with him. And he said, Let me go, for the day breaketh. And he said, I will not let thee go, except thou bless me. And he said unto him, What is thy name? And he said, Jacob. And he said, Thy name shal be called no more Jacob, but Israel; for as a prince hast thou power with God and with men, and hast prevailed. And Jacob asked him and said, Tell me I pray thee, thy name. And he said, Wherefore is it that thou dost ask after my name? And he blessed him there. And Jacob called the name ot the place Peniel, for I have seen God face to face, and my life is preserved.

GEN. XXXII. 24-30.

THE VICTORY OF DEFEAT.

Each for himself that desolate vale must tread,
    No mortal man his brother may redeem
From the lone hour's despondency and dread;
    No costly ransom price procure for him.

There is set up the solemn judgment seat,
    Immunity from which we thought to win;
Tho' thro' long years our conscience we should cheat,
    Inexorably confronted with our sin.

The blood-avenger vengeance may delay,
    But the respite mistake not for reprieve,—
Breaks to the birth the inevitable day,
    When we the heaped-up penalty receive.

When, sore amazed and saddened e'en to death,
    Gethsemane's momentous hour draws near,
In vain we summon, as with parting breath,
    Familiar friends and intimates most dear—

To watch with us through the wild night of woe,—
  Their sense is holden that they cannot see
Nor feel the presence of the infernal foe,
  The grapple of the last great agony,—

When, in God's wine-press crushed, the heart's life blood
  Flows freely forth, and streams of blinding tears,
Shed with strong cries, our nightly pillow flood—
  Crowded in one short hour the grief of years.

II

Thus, at the brink of Jabbok's storied brook,
    For Israel strikes life's fateful crisis-hour;
Profoundly dark the perilous outlook—
    Dread Nemesis asserting her fell power.

Expecting when with dawning day shall fall
    Destruction fell on us and all we love,
Nor seeing how the disaster to forestall,—
    Driven desperate we cast our eyes above:

Encountered suddenly by one like man—
  Distincter form the gloom gives not to see—
Quivers the question on our lips all wan,
  " Art thou for us or our adversary ? "

Whose are the arms thus violently seize
  With unrelenting grasp our trembling frame ?
Whose this chill breath the vital stream might freeze ?
  What mischievous, malign intent his aim ?

For that aught else than malice could inspire
  So sharp an onset—past conception seems ;—
'Twas sure some eye aflame with vengeful ire
  Thro' the thick gloom shot those fierce angry gleams.

Like Laocoon caught in the encircling coil
  Of monstrous snakes wreathed round each writhing limb ;—
Those limbs to extricate all vain his toil,
  Or rid him of the rueful horror grim,—

THE VICTORY OF DEFEAT.

Thus wrestle we with ruthless Destiny,
    As it appears to our distracted thought ;
From high designs of love would set us free,
    But all our desperate efforts came to nought,—

Till—on the stronghold of our proud self-will
    Falls irresistibly the stroke divine ;
The broken heart lies passive now and still,
    Nor of continued struggle gives a sign,—

But takes to her embrace the suspected foe—
    The adversary proving her best friend—
Finds healing in the bitter fount of woe,
    Seeing to what blest goal her labours tend.

The hand, whose palsying touch upon us lies,
    Is that of matchless love's omnipotence ;—
Tho' nature's courage 'neath its pressure dies,
    The higher good springs from *her* indigence.

III.

The strong man arméd keeps his house in peace,
    Intact his substance, till the stronger one
Against him comes, breaks thro' his edifice,
    Parts the rapt spoil, his fond defence undone.

Entrenched in worldly trust, at ease we cry:—
" Soul, thou hast goods laid up for many years;
In the warm shelter of my nest I'll lie,
    Away with doubt and melancholy fears!

" Have I not for my pleasure and renown
    This palace built me scatheless shall endure?
On other folk misfortune fell may frown,
    In fearless freedom I'll abide secure."

THE VICTORY OF DEFEAT.

And—while the word is yet upon our lips—
   A watcher and a holy one is by,
To summon the disastrous storm that strips
   Our boughs, and with the branchage strews the
      sky ;—

" Hew down the tree, waste the well-laden boughs !
   Shake off the leaf, and scatter wide the fruit !
No longer 'neath its shade the beast shall browse,
   Nor herd for shelter gather round its root ;—

" Yet leave the stump—that with the dew of heaven
   And scent of moisture it may yet revive ;
Beauty and strength again to it be given
   When the long-tarrying spring-time shall arrive ;

" When, lessoned in humiliation's school,
   Brute folly to humaner thoughts gives place ;
Till humbly he confess the Heavens to rule,
   And in the dust his lofty looks abase."

IV.

So resolute are set the eternal powers
   To stain the arrogance of human pride,—
Casting to earth each haughty thought that towers
   Vain-gloriously, the vaunts high heaven defied.

Yet all that they design from us to reave,
   Divested of, our state were happier far:
More prudent grown such things we gladly leave—
   Impediments the spirit's progress bar—

The spurious, fleshly hopes that close the way
   Against the entrance of the supreme good,—
Gross sensuous bonds the spirit that delay
   The blinded prisoner of the passions lewd.

So they address them to their desperate task,
    Prepared to spoil all we esteem most dear,—
Their gracious purpose hiding 'neath the mask
    Of angered hate the spirit fills with fear :—

The prison, not the prisoner there entombed
    They band them with full intent to destroy
He—to a lingering hopeless bondage doomed—
    Sound of beginning battle greets with joy.

V.

Thus wrestled they with him renowned of yore—
    A perfect man and upright in his way,
When wave on wave of trouble on him bore,
    Till, in his bitterness, he cursed his day :—

"Let the day perish wherein I was born!
    The night wherein a man-child was conceived!
May no divine regard greet that dark morn,
    Its blackness by no star-shine be relieved!—

" Since it closed not the cruel gates of life,
    Nor shut the portals of my mother's womb,
'Gainst me—sad wretch! whose years with ills are rife,
    Whom swift misfortune hurries to the tomb.

THE VICTORY OF DEFEAT.

" For tranquil now and peaceful had I lain,
    Buried in sleep of utter nothingness;
Like some untimely birth, a mother's pain
    Ne'er compensates with infantile caress.

" There— from their sore annoy the prisoners rest,
    The proud-oppressor's voice no more they hear;
The small and great with equal peace are blest,
    The slave is freed for ever from his fear.

" As the worn warrior waits the welcome day,
    From warfare's hard fatigue shall bring release;
Or hireling-hind the evening's growing grey,
    From labour's heat and burden gives surcease, —

" So eagerly I greet the lingering hour,
    Shall grant me sweet relief from my long pain,
Clear the thick clouds o'er my sad pathway lower,
    And the dark mystery of life explain.

" Man that is woman-born hath but few days,
 Yet are those days of feverish trouble full ;
Flower-like he flourisheth, but never stays
 The same,—the fleeting hours his hopes annul.

" Why is light given men steeped in misery?
 And life those vexed with bitterness of soul?
Who crave for death—but unavailingly,
 To whom oblivion seems a blissful goal ;—

" Rejoicing with a joy exceeding great,
 When, after painful quest, they find the grave ;
With courage and new-quickened hope elate,
 The horrors of the tomb prepared to brave.

" For now the Almighty's arrows drink my blood,
 His terrors are arrayed against my soul,
He breaketh in upon me, like a flood
 Bursting its banks, defiant of control.

THE VICTORY OF DEFEAT.

" What am I that thine eye my path should scan,
    Nor e'er permit me to escape its gaze ?—
Perpetually subject to thy ban,
    That still the threatened fateful stroke delays.

" I said of Sheol :—' There would I abide,
    In her cold gloomy chambers gladly dwell !
Corruption choose as my espoused bride,
    The worm's companionship shall please me well ! '

" Wilt thou not there in secrecy conceal
    Me—till thy time of wrath be overpast,—
When, at the last dread trump's terrific peal,
    The amazed and startled heavens shall stand aghast !

" Lo ! I go forward—but he is not there,
    And backward—but his steps I cannot trace
His ear is deaf to my importunate prayer,
    He veils in vengeance his averted face !

" My path is fencéd that I cannot pass,
    And thickest darkness fallen upon my way ;
His troops press on me in dense serried mass,
    And round my tent their bannered lines display ! "

VI.

Thus in the vexed, perturbèd human breast
  Deep hoarsely calls to deep, and wave to wave,—
A troubled sea whose waters cannot rest,
  But wildly and incontinently rave,—

Till He appear who stills the sea's proud rage,
  And maketh quiet where prevailed the storm,—
The tempest in man's spirit to assuage,
  And to tranquility its wrath transform;—

Till God, arising in the majesty
  Of awful holiness and matchless might,—
To teach his fretful child humility,
  Enrobe him in the insufferable light.

THE VICTORY OF DEFEAT.

All we most valued proves illusive good,
    Virtue's proud semblance to corruption turns,—
As the keen fire-flame kindled in the wood—
    Withered and dry—quick thro' its substance burns.

Needs but a word, a breath, a glance divine
    Befall the baseless fabric of man's pride,—
Our vain self-confidence to undermine,
    Till from their crown the crumbling ruins slide;—

Needs but that the Almighty's finger point
    To some small part of his stupendous ways,—
Our arrogant self-trust is out of joint,
    Prostrated we adore in silent praise:—

VII

" Where, when the huge foundations of the earth
    Were laid, was thine abode, what thine employ ?—
The morning stars were jubilant with mirth,
    Loud shouted all the sons of God for joy.

" When the sea issued forth as from the womb,
    And from her swaddling bands young ocean brake,
Didst thou spread o'er her the thick shrouding gloom?
    Or of the dark a sable mantle make?

" Didst thou impose a stablished sure decree,
    Forbidding her to pass the appointed bound?—
The restless, vast, ungovernable sea
    Within strait bars and doors didst thou impound?—

" Piling in heaps the innumerable sands
    To curb her uncontrollable brute rage,
Lest the proud surges should usurp the lands,
    And claim them as their proper appanage?

" Arcturus' path in heaven hast thou defined,
    Or thro' the twelve signs led the advancing Sun?
The Pleiades' sweet influence canst thou bind?
    Or loose the mighty bands of Orion?

" Hast thou the morn commanded since thy days?
    Or made the springing dawn to know its place,—
When, breaking thro' the obscure eclipsing haze,
    The day's bright orb speeds on its wonted race.

" Knowest thou how the bony framework knits
    Within the womb of one that is with child?
How member to its fellow-member fits,
    Till all-complete the bodily-structure's piled?

" How, day by day, in the hid inward part,
    Continually they were fashioned—one by one ;
And wrought in secret with most cunning art—
    ·Long ere thy life-career commenced to run ? "

VIII.

If thus from thy close search remains concealed
    The workmanship divine in vulgar clay,
How should the deeper mystery be revealed
    Thy spirit's birth and growth that underlay?

Who guides the planetary spheres thro' space,
    Aberrant tho' their orbit oft appear,
Thy path thro' time's bare wild with care doth trace,
    Life's labyrinthine maze to him shines clear.

THE VICTORY OF DEFEAT.

The spirit's closely-sealed imprisoning tomb,
   Wrapt in sepulchral gloom of foulest night,
What is it but an all-prolific womb —
   Profusely sown with pregnant germs of light?—

Laboratory where creative skill
   With patience fabricates her works sublime,
And renders all-subservient to her will
   The dark events crowd the rude scroll of time?

From earth's crude moral chaos He can raise—
   Rich in resources of omnipotence—
A fair, well ordered world, from whence his praise
   Shall mount like odours of sweet frankincense

Subtle the process by which Supreme Love
   Moulds to its perfect form the immortal soul;—
And to high ends doth things untoward move,
   Submitting them to its complete control.

He who its boundaries for the ocean sets,
    And curbs the unbridled fury of the main,—
The barriers against which thy proud will frets
    Ordained—thy restless passions to restrain :—

Hitherto—but no further—shall they reach,
    These pains assign the bounds to their wild sway ;
And patient self-control so sternly preach—
    Rebellious nature must perforce obey.

IX.

If, from the heart of whirlwind, flame, and storm,
    The Lord address him to our discontent,
And, framing his demands in such-like form,
    Enter with us into high argument,—

O'erpowered, as the prince of Judah's seers
    In presence of the fiery seraph choir,
Ranged round the argent throne in dazzling tiers,
    We cry—faint, undone, ready to expire :—

" Now that my eyes have looked upon the Lord—
    The Judge of all the earth, pure, holy, just—
My soul henceforth is of itself abhorred,
    Abased I bow before thee in the dust ;—

THE VICTORY OF DEFEAT.

" Thou hast chastised me and I was chastised—
    A bullock unaccustomed to the yoke :—
With troubles sore and labours exercised—
    My stubborn temper yet remained unbroke.

" Now I abandon every vain device;
    That stiff-necked beast—blind, obstinate self-will—
I freely yield thee up a sacrifice,
    Its life-blood spare thou not but wholly spill."

X.

" OH, that my wiser, better thoughts were penned
    In lasting record on the lettered page !
That iron style and lead their aid might lend
    My words to carry to a distant age !

" Tho' He should slay me yet in him I'll trust,
    From the foul grave my hope shall spring more
        pure ;
A foiled antagonist—from the low dust
    Invigorate I shall rise—of victory sure ;—

" From out my weakness grow exceeding strong,
    More valiant wax as speeds the desperate fight ;
Then raise aloft my glorious pæan-song
    Loudest when thickest falls the gloom of night.

"Thou my redeemer art, for me thou liv'st,
   To stand at last my daysman on this earth!
Tho' my worn flesh a prey to worms thou giv'st,
   Thro' the waste shell the spirit breaks to birth:

"All freed from blinding film, gross veil of sense,
   Base slavish fear made me thy face to shun,—
I'll gain the spiritual Pisgah whence
   The beatific vision shall be won.

"Though amid worldly joys complete surcease,
   Of evil days and few my pilgrimage—
I reck not, nor tho' 'gainst my present peace
   The powers of earth and hell conspire to rage.

"If, a lone outcast, I again embrace
   The rock for shelter—with the naked stone
For pillow,—from this solitary place
   Ascend the steps conducting to thy throne.

" Each desert scene my way-worn feet have trod,
  From home and hope, from friends and comfort driven,
 I recognise to be the very house of God,
  The gateway and the portal of high heaven."

XI.

Thus the day breaks, the shadows flee away,
    The fair bright dawn reveals with whom we've striven,—
No power malign, with purpose fell to slay,
    But a commissioned messenger from heaven :—

No fiend from the abyss, but from above
    A friend, a tried well-proven auxiliary,
Charged with most blest designs of wondrous love,
    Tho' wrought thro' pain's ungentle ministry :

Changes our fear to joy and rapt surprise,
    And eagerness to win the boon he brings ;
No longer for release the spirit cries,
    But to this gracious friend and helper clings ;—

Clings—for to wrestle longer power hath none ;—
    Since that miraculous touch was on us laid—
All nature's strength is ruined and undone,
    The pillars of self-confidence decayed.

So the disciples on vexed Galilee—
    Convulsed by sudden violence of storm,
Blind with pale terror, knew not it was he
    They loved, conceiving some grim ghostly form,—

When, in the fourth watch of that wakeful night,
    For their relief and help he walked the wave,—
Appalled by so unparallelled a sight,
    Not thus expecting his approach to save.

The whispered accents : "Fear not, it is I !"
    Their spirits' wild affright at once allay :—
"Lo ! I would come !" is Peter's quick reply,
    "Tho' thro' the leaping billows lie my way."

THE VICTORY OF DEFEAT.

Still are we troubled—entering the cloud
  Irradiate from the bright Shekinah-shrine;
The tabernacle of the Blessèd seems our shroud,
  We shudder, called to share in bliss divine:—

Let but the curtain lift, the silence break,
  Our suffering Lord unveil his face all fair,—
On the lone mount our home we now would make,
  For nowhere is it good for us but there.

XII.

His garment the blind beggar flings away
    That to the gracious healer he may press ;—
Well pleased the spirit feels the flesh decay,
    And gladly parts with its gross cumbrous dress,—

That she may closely press, and firmly hold
    To the Great Spirit near to her akin ;
And—with new-wakened faith, resolved and bold,
    Will not let go till she the blessing win :—

" I will not let Thee go !" I base my claim
    Upon no strength or merit of my own,
But—for that to the claims of the weak and lame
    Those of the proud and strong thou dost postpone.

THE VICTORY OF DEFEAT.

"I will not hide my guiltiness and shame,
    My nakedness and need shun not to tell,—
Transgressor from the womb my rightful name,
    Conceived beneath sin's dark unholy spell:

"E'en when thy favour and thy grace I sued,
    The birthright and the blessing strove to win,—
My very goodness was itself not good,
    But tainted with immedicable sin :

"I claim as birthright now the blessing given
    To souls submissive, penitent, and meek,—
Heart-broken suppliants whom the King of heaven
    As the recipients of his grace doth seek.

"Within the precincts of thy sacred courts,
    E'en on the outcast poor thy grace bestows
A place and name, whose signature imports
    Greater degree than son or daughter knows.

THE VICTORY OF DEFEAT.

" The lowliest task within thy temple, Lord,
    Tho' but to keep its door, I humbly claim,
Which glimpses of thy glory shall afford,
    Where I may spell the secret of thy name.

" In the fair courts by saintly victors trod
    E'en I may dwell, and glad Hosannas raise,—
A pillar in the temple of my God,
    A trophy storied with thy fame and praise !

" Endue me from henceforth with kingly power
    O'er my base self the mastery to wield ;
In this sublime, high consecrated hour,
    Knight me, my Liege ! upon the battle-field.

" The battle-field shall be my Peniel ;
    There—where I met Jehovah face to face—
The Jacob died, to rise an Israel,
    The prince the shrewd supplanter did displace.

EPILOGUE.

Periods of sickness ever mark the growth
   Of increased faculty and added power ;
The crisis most reluctantly and loath
   We enter—proves the spirit's natal hour.

The new ideal with its large demands—
   Seeing that we have nought wherewith to pay—
With weakness, and with imperfection, brands
   Our most successful, best designed essay :

The higher life the spirit brooding o'er
   With its excessive light makes dark our day,
While—amid anguish wild, and labour sore—
   It new creates, and glorifies our clay :

THE VICTORY OF DEFEAT.

When the high heavenly powers overshade,
    And move on us—as erst on chaos rude—
Fear-stricken is the heart, and all-dismayed,
    Perplexed with horror and incertitude,—

Not knowing that these inward stirrings deep,
    These throes wherewith the struggling soul is torn,
Our strong outcries, the bitter tears we weep,
    Tell of the holy thing now being born.

'Tis when deliverance approacheth near
    In agonised suspense the spirit hangs,
E'en as a woman in her pain and fear
    Groaneth aloud for her sore travail pangs.

Exceeding troubled we are fain to cry,
    As the near trial hour we realise,
Spare me at any cost this agony !
    Let me but live—who will may take the prize ;—

Till borne the thought with strong resistless force
    Upon the hesitating shrinking will—
That only in this shunned, abhorréd course
    Life's true and lofty purpose we fulfil.

O wretched man ! this flesh, this bodily death
    Put off, its false and clamorous claims eschew !
And let the Spirit's generous quickening breath
    With larger, fuller life thy being's source renew.

SUSPIRIA.

Ps. LXXXIV.

SUSPIRIA.

Lord of Hosts ! enthroned in glory !
Beauteous are thy courts above,
Where the ransomed saints the story
Utter of thy boundless love ;
Towards thy dwelling
All my deepest passions move.

Sore unrest my spirit aileth,—
Whence this inward sharp distress ?
Heart and flesh together faileth
While, thro' earth's drear wilderness,
To thine altars
Ardently my soul doth press.

Happy birds within the precinct
    Of those altars that abide,
Led by sure unerring instinct
    'Neath thy sheltering wings to hide,
        With the central
    Source and seat of bliss allied!

Happy they, who, like them dwelling
    Ever in the heavenly courts,
Still the rapturous tale are telling
    The enravished sense transports!
        Each new vision
    Of the King fresh praise extorts.

There the plentiful rich treasures
    Of his temple are displayed;
With the river of his pleasures
    Is their feverish thirst allayed;
        There the splendent
Glory-sheen dispels all shade.

By the cool clear crystal waters—
  Making glad thy house—a name
Better than of sons and daughters
  'Tis their high proud boast to claim ;
    How the prospect
  Does the glowing heart inflame!

They partake a kindred blessing—
  The undaunted pilgrim band,
Who with girded loins are pressing
  To the glory-lighted land,
    Aye obedient
  To thine outstretched, guiding hand.

Passing thro' the vale ot sorrow
  Springeth there for them a fount,
Vigour from whose wave they borrow
  As on eagle's wings to mount :
    Vale of Baca—
  Vale of blessing they account !

SUSPIRIA.

From their eyes the copious tear-shower,
  Shed full oft upon life's way,
Filled their cup,—but added power
  In the bitter potion lay :
    Ever found they
Help sufficient for their day,—

Still increasing strength in weakness
  Of the suffering fleshly frame,
Whose perfected fruit was meekness
  In endurance; thro' the name
    Of the victor-
Victim Lamb they overcame.

They, thro' pressure of temptation
  To full spirit-stature grown,
Take their fitting, rightful station
  Near the effulgent, fiery throne,—
    Rays thence streaming
For all sufferings atone.

With the Lamb upon Mount Zion,
  'Mid the blood-bought martyr host,
Now they stand,—hell's prowling lion
  Faileth to make good his boast—
    From God's hand to
Pluck them ; not e'en one is lost.

One day in thy courts is better
  Than a thousand spent elsewhere ;
Freed from each enthralling fetter,
  With the ransomed let me share
    Thy blest vision,
Breathe heaven's clear, fresh, vital air !

On the face of thine anointed
  Let thy heavenly favour shine !
Perfect now the work appointed,
  Manifest the face divine !
    To thy servant's
Passionate request incline !

Thou whose strong right hand of power
    Still supports the faint and frail ;
Who, in life's dread peril hour,
    Mad'st the patriarch prevail,—
        Thou hast promised :
    " Jacob's face shall ne'er wax pale !"

When my night of strife is ended,
    May I, like thine Israel,
Learn that life's long conflict tended
    To an eternal Peniel :
        If with morning-
Dawn I see thee—all is well !

Let me but behold the beauty
    Of thy countenance, my Lord!—
Some low place of humble duty,
    Which shall but a glimpse afford
        Of thy glory,
Let thy grace to me accord!

If my heart but there have leisure
    On thy love to meditate,—
Let who will have worldly pleasure,
    Wealth, vain pomp, and high estate;
        This suffices—
At thy doors to stand and wait;—

Catch some far faint transient gleaming
    From the throne's clear crystalline,
Some bright lustrous beam outstreaming
    From the blest Shekinah-shrine;—
        All I ask for,
All I can desire is mine.

Sheltered by the Almighty power—
  Trouble may not reach me there ;
In the baleful peril-hour
  Thou thy strong right arm wilt bare ;
    Thou wilt snatch me
  From the tempter's siren snare.

For the Lord a sun and shield is
  In our darkness and distress ;
Wondrously hath he revealed his
  Grace our sorrows to redress ;
    Glory waits us—
  Safely passed life's wilderness.

Nought of good shall be with-holden
  From the single-eyed and true,
This should pilgrim hearts embolden
  Who Christ's bleeding track pursue ;
    Press we onward
  With the vision bright in view !

THE CORRECTED ESTIMATE.

Ps. LXXIII.

THE CORRECTED ESTIMATE.

Truly the Lord is good to Israel—
Men single-minded and of guileless heart;
Surely it shall be with the righteous well,
    Tho' frequent grief's quick smart:

But, as for me, my feet had almost gone,
My treadings slipt beneath me, when I saw
The prosperous ease of the ungodly one,
    Unmoved by shame or awe.

Compassed are they, close-wrapped about with pride,
And fenced with fierceness and rude insolence;
They haughtily above our bowed heads ride,
    Be-mock our innocence:

Their eyes with fatness swell, beyond their hope
Succeed their schemes of craft and villainy;
Against High Heaven their scornful lips they ope
    In bitter blasphemy.

Then said I : 'Twas in vain I cleansed my heart,
And practised purity in word and deed :—
Their's is the happier lot, the better part,
    The more convenient creed.

For I am stricken sore the whole day long,
My chastisement begins with each new morn;
Upon my back the smiters laid the thong,
    Deep were the furrows worn.

In the confused and multitudinous sea
Of my vexed thoughts I strove to understand
These things;—they proved an unsolved mystery,
    Refusing to be scanned,—

Till, at the last, my inly-burning heat
Had well nigh broken forth incontinent
In frantic words; my heart, with grief replete,
    Found fierce and angry vent :—

Thy dealings with thy people all forgot—
As upward-mounting sparks to trouble born—
With the blaspheming crew had cast my lot,
    Sat amongst men that scorn.

But when thy sanctuary's courts I trod,
And graduated in that sacred school,—
The gloom grew luminous in Thy light, O God,
    To me, poor purblind fool!

Fell from mine eyes as it had been thick scales—
Hid the prospective vision from my view;
My spirit pierced the interposing veils
    The flesh around it drew.

THE CORRECTED ESTIMATE.

No longer on the apparent was my gaze
Now fixed, nor lingered on the present scene:—
The vain show penetrating, deep amaze
    Replaced my envious spleen,—

Surprise and horror—for that giddy height,
On which I too had gladly stood, appeared,—
Its glittering splendour and repute despite,
    For pride's destruction reared.

Life's high conspicuous summits now seemed fraught
With peril,—slippery the paths they tread,
At glory's phantom eagerly who caught,
    Their baffled grasp still fled

Swift as the images the dreamer views,
In ceaseless, quick succession hurrying by,
That for one moment the conceit amuse,
    Then mock the trusting eye.

THE CORRECTED ESTIMATE.

The bitter thoughts wherewith my spirit eyed
Their grandeur and short lived prosperity,
Sprang from my brutish foolishness and pride,
    My gross fatuity.

Yet doth this crude, blind, senseless ignorance
But lay the stronger claim on thy kind care,—
Of thy regard, guidance, and maintenance
    I need the greater share.

Holden by thy right hand, and by thine eye
Counselled, and led along life's lowlier way,—
Henceforth I would refrain from thoughts too high,
    As a weaned child obey ;

And following where my gracious Shepherd leads
The least sagacious of his tended train,—
The living founts, the rich, green, fruitful meads
    Of heaven's glad pastures gain :

There feed my spirit with the prospect fair
Of beauty ne'er shall pall, nor fade away;
Breathe of the still, clear, pure, celestial air,
    Bathe in unclouded day!

The Lord Himself is my inheritance,
My everlasting portion; well the lines
Have fallen me by his loving ordinance;
    My heart no more repines.

Whom have I in the Paradise above
E'en for a moment to compare with thee!
The earthly idols I had given my love
    Proved less than vanity.

Henceforth let earth's fond pleasures fade and fail;
My heart and flesh decline, all comforts die:—
Rent thereby is each intercepting veil
    Eclipsed thee to mine eye.

I glory in the weakness that ensures
The power divine shall overshadow me,—
Since 'tis my very helplessness secures
    Thy gracious sympathy.

THE QUIETED SOUL

Ps. CXXXI.

THE QUIETED SOUL.

No longer shall my heart be lifted up,
    As in my foolish wayward youth ;
Since I have drunk of grief's gall-mingled cup
    My soul is filled with ruth.

I exercise myself no more with things too great—
    Above the range of mortal ken,—
But high conceits, and thoughts with pride elate,
    Within just limits pen ;

THE QUIETED SOUL.

Stilling and quieting my weanéd soul,
      Lest back again to earth it turn,—
And—breaking from thy loving, wise control—
      With new-lit passion burn :

Lest once more seeking its forsaken nest—
      The home of its nativity,
It there search vainly for content and rest
      Where such can never be.

By life's unfathomable, boundless sea
      I mutely take my humble stand,—
Well pleased its turbulent billows bow to thee,
      Submit to thy command ;—

And, prostrate in admiring wonder, cry :—
      " In silence art thou best adored !
In vain man's purblind wisdom seeks to pry
      Into thy thoughts, O Lord ! "

In presence of life's mysteries that fill
    The heart with manifold alarms,—
Let me but feel outstretched beneath me still
    The everlasting arms!

Set thou, O Israel! on the Lord thy trust,
    In childlike, meek simplicity;
The Judge of all the earth, most true and just,
    Rules in strict equity.

THE PURPOSE OF THE AGES.

Rom. viii. 17-39.

THE PURPOSE OF THE AGES.

I.

CHILDREN since He deigns to call us—
   Joint-heirs with the first-born child,
What though desolate before us
   Glooms our pathway o'er life's wild!
Small earth's anguish when contrasted
   With the glory we shall wear,
When the image of the heavenly
   In our souls stands outlined clear;
When all cleansed from earth's accretions—
   Veiling from us the divine,
We shall stand in the High Presence,
   With the reflex lustre shine;
Proving how these present sufferings
   Served our nature to refine:

Proving to what spirit freedom
   Creaturehood may yet attain—
What a wealth of holy treasure
   E'en the least endowed may gain—
How exceeding rich the harvest
   Won from soil bedewed with pain.

Looking for such high ideal
   Cranes the creature the stretched neck,
As despairing seamen gather
   On the spar-strewn, wave-swept deck,
Eyes upraised for help and rescue
   From some hapless, desperate wreck:
Waiting for the manifesting
   Of the new born sons of light,
For the young, bright, fair immortals
   Who shall turn the tide of fight,—
Carve a pathway thro' the darkness
   Of earth's drear, disastrous night.

II.

Knowest thou not how all creation
   Groans in travail pangs till now,
'Neath her awful entailed burden
   Thro' long ages forced to bow!
Nature throbs with expectation,
   Thrills of hope shoot through the sphere,
Broods o'er earth the conscious feeling
   Her glad dawn is drawing near;
Presaging this age-long travail
   Pregnant with some purpose great,
Some grand birth of peerless splendour
   For her pains to compensate:
Waiting when the new-create heaven
   Shall disclose itself to view,

And the earth, a bride impatient,
    Clothe her in apparel new,
Robes of brightness and of beauty
    For her sackcloth mean indue.

We, within whose hearts are working
    Powers of the world to come,
Migratory instincts yearning
    To the spirit's native home,—
Eager hopes and aspirations
    Wing us for our heavenward flight,
Sadly call we each to other
    As we cleave the gulf of night,
Wintry cold and gloom forsaking
    For fair climes of cloudless light :—
With the grand redemptive movement
    Linked in closest sympathy—
Through us all earth's labouring birth-throes
    Vibrate with intensity ;
Feel we every thrill and throbbing—
    For upon the heart and brain

Of each sentient organism
  Chiefly falls the stress and strain,
And each more developed member
  Is most sensitive to pain.

Soiled investiture from off us,
  Oh! how gladly would we fling,
The defilement to the fleshly
  Seems inseparably to cling!
That, apparelled in pure raiment,
  Leaders in the foremost van,
We might speed the mighty movement,
  The triumphal march of man ;
Freed ourselves—assist our fellows
  To fling off sin's fatal ban.

All-reluctantly the creature
  Was involved in vanity,
Every young and budding purpose
  Nipped in immaturity ;
Hopes and instincts baulked and blighted,
  Schemes most cherished brought to nought,

Efforts baffled and abortive,
  With defeat and failure fraught ;
None as yet of all her children
  Her deliverance has wrought :
Looks she for some strong redeemer
  From her bale to set her free,
Of a nobler generation
  " Promise, type, and potency,"
Opening and inaugurating
  Earth's blest age of jubilee.

III.

Full of glad anticipation
  Of this glory yet to rise,
Moved to ecstacy the prophet
  Cries in rapturous surprise :—
" Unto us is born a man-child,
  Unto us a son is given,
And from off our neck from henceforth
  The oppressor's yoke is riven :
On his shoulder lies the burden
  Of the broad earth's government,
In his name earth's highest titles
  Into unity are blent."

Incommunicable titles
  If for most part those he bears--

That of the elect and first-born
    With his brethren he shares ;
For he stamps his likeness on them,
    Making them the sons of God—
Leads them by the self-same pathway
    He their forerunner has trod ;
Sanctifies himself for their sake,
    That they, instinct with his truth,
Consecrate themselves for others,
    For in them he sees the youth
Of the yet victorious manhood,
    Who, thro' him unite with them,
The disastrous tide of evil
    Shall have strength at last to stem.

That which Israel failed to accomplish
    This new Israel shall effect,
Antitype of ancient Israel,
    For this purpose high elect ;
Graft of the wild olive planted
    In their place by God reject.

IV.

Strange new thoughts are kindled in us
  At the rapt prophetic word,
Scarcely conscious whither tending
  The emotions in us stirred:
Dimly seen, stupendous visions
  Flit before the gaze of hope,—
All in vain we seek to master
  Their significance and scope.
Thus is left us room for yearnings
  Vast and vague, for faith and prayer,
Auguries and aspirations
  Which to utter scarce we dare.

Little know we what petitions
  To the throne supreme to send,

What conditions would most further
    The attaining of our end ;—
So we give us to the Spirit,
    Pray that he may trim the sail,
Take the helm, assume the guidance,
    Send the favouring, speeding gale ;
'Gainst the opposing floods of evil
    Give us power to prevail.

With the Will Divine accordant
    He within us intercedes,
And interprets the expression
    Scarce articulate of our needs ;
While—harmonious with his workings,
    And the mind of the Supreme,
All events are that befall us,
    How untoward soe'er they seem ;
Aid we hardly could dispense with,
    They in turn successive lend,
Each and all co-operating
    The divinely purposed end.

V.

Their's from earthly dross and grossness
   Thy rude spirit to refine,
Make a living, real experience
   The Great Artist's high design:
The idea ever present
   To the everlasting will,
This—thy life's inspired ideal—
   At all cost he must fulfil.

Call to mind the things in vision
   Manifested on the Mount,
In the moments when thy spirit
   Soared to love's own living fount!

When the pattern there was shown thee
    Of the heavenly sanctuary,
The pure shrine, where the full Godhead
    Dwells with man perpetually.

What this earth but the rude quarry,
    Whence the shapely stones are hewn,
To be placed each in due order
    In its destined niche full soon?
Here the din of tool and hammer,
    Seeming waste and foul debris,—
There the all-fair fabric riseth
    Noiseless and harmoniously—
Light affliction for the moment
    Of life's brief and passing day,
By the antagonistic forces
    Round us now which freely play,
Working out a nobler structure
    'Neath this crumbling house of clay

VI.

This the purpose we were called for—
  Wholly to be filled with love,
In our measure reproducing
  The all-perfect type above
Flaming seraph, fair bright cherub,
  Type of the Incarnate Son,—
Of the many to come after
  The Elect, the First-born one.
Man of sorrows eminently,
  And through life acquaint with grief,
Of his character the features
  How bring out in full relief,
Otherwise than by submitting
  To the process keen of pain,
Which the hand of the great sculptor
  To perform on us may deign?
This his glorious purpose for us
  None can hinder nor frustrate;—
For its perfect realisation
  From before time consecrate,—
Every birth of time must surely
  Its fulfilment mediate.

VII.

Ere He laid earth's dark foundations,
    Firmly fixed its corner stone,
When as yet dwelt the Omniscient
    In his majesty alone ;
In the prime, the first dim dawning
    Of his ways, when not as yet
On the lawless main his measuring
    Line and compass had been set,—
While the heavens were yet preparing,
    The clear crystal firmament,
Ere the upper, nether waters
    Were within strait limits pent ;—
Ere the mighty mountain summits
    Were upheaven from the deep,—
When no form minutest, meanest,
    In the dust of earth did creep ;—

THE PURPOSE OF THE AGES.

In his all-foreknowing counsels,
   Ere these labour pangs of earth,
Thou—his latest, last creation—
   Had'st already come to birth :
Present even then thy concept,
   Fully, perfectly defined,
In completest detail imaged,
   Stood before the Eternal Mind.

For his keen, all-prescient wisdom
   Pierced the chaos wild and rude—
The preparatory periods—
   Teeming with the uncouth and crude,
Till its penetrating vision
   Rested with supreme delight
On the earth fresh-won from chaos,
   And the dark domain of night ;
Fully satisfied it rested
   Upon all within its ken,
But its keenest joy was wakened
   By the world of ransomed men—

THE PURPOSE OF THE AGES.

Fair bright world the darkening shadow
   Flung by sin no longer haunts,
Peopled to its utmost borders
   With pure holy habitants,—
Final aim of his creation,
   Goal towards which all things tend,
Apex of the complex structure,
   Whither all the steps ascend ;
Of immensely greater import
   Than the means must be the end.

VIII.

Each from each inseparable
  Are the links of the great chain
Which connect thy mean beginning
  With the heights thou yet shalt gain;
Marshalled for thee stand the forces
  Of the Lord Omnipotent,
Of the God who called thee, chose thee,
  On thy service all intent,
Lest thy feet should slide or stumble,
  For thy help and succour sent.
No array of angry foemen
  Should affright thee or appal,—
Chariots and horsemen many
  Gird thee like a flaming wall.
Grace and glory he'll provide thee,
  Here—upon thy pilgrim way,
When the flesh and spirit faileth,
  Be thy strong support and stay;
There,—the splendour of his presence
  Sheds its full refulgent ray.

IX.

GREATEST gift ensures the lesser,—
　He who gave for thee his son,
Of all other gifts thou needest
　Grudgeth nor withholdeth one.
Who a charge shall lay against thee?
　The divine judicature
Hath already sealed thy pardon,
　Thy acquittal then is sure.

Thou a brand plucked from the burning,
　Charred and blackened by the flame,
In thine own eyes foul and loathsome,
　Child of misery and shame,—
Freed from all that long hath made thee
　To thyself a thing abhorred,
Clad in fair and priestly beauty
　Yet shalt stand before thy Lord,
With the sanctities of heaven
　All thy being in accord!

X.

One with Christ thou'st died and risen,
  Flung thy baser self away,—
Life eternal greets thy spirit,
  Welcomes thee to cloudless day.
There the mystic Christ abideth
  Of whom thou art now a part,—
Flows the life blood to each member
  From the central, living heart:
Since the breach between the human
  And divine hath been atoned,—
In the seat of supreme power
  Thy humanity's enthroned.
As the stream blends its glad waters
  With the great unfathomed sea,
Ransomed souls their being mingle
  With the all-glorious Deity.
Spirit union disunites not
  At the touch of mortal thing,—
Pain, distress, or tribulation,
  Nakedness, or famishing,—
Over all thou art victorious,
  Vanquished for thee is their sting

XI.

Though the fig-tree fail to blossom,
   No fruit grace the blighted vine,
Waste the labour given the olive,
   Tho' all grass and herbage pine;
Tho' no flock at eve be folded,
   Idle stand the empty stall,—
In our God we joy and glory,
   In his love possess we all!

Sharpest sword or deadliest peril
   Cannot part the living cord,
By which, in life's bundle, loving
   Men are bound with love's own Lord!
Nay, I doubt not, all such mischiefs
   But defeat their own design,
And the spirit-bond draw closer
   'Twixt the human and divine,
Love from earth's vain hopes thus severed
   Round eternal hope doth twine.

XII.

Hurl we then a proud defiance
  At all forms of outward ill!—
They but execute the purpose
  Of the Everlasting Will,
Which, for highest ends to fashion
  All adverse events, hath skill.
Life and death, angelic powers,
  Mightiest principalities,
Present things and things yet future,
  Heights and depths through all degrees,—
But assist the struggling creature
  To attain its perfect birth,
Consummate the evolution
  Of the promised heavens and earth;
Thro' such painful process only
  Is accomplished aught of worth.

THE ETERNAL REFUGE.

Ps. xc.

THE ETERNAL REFUGE.

I.

THROUGHOUT all generations, thou, O Lord !
   A refuge sure hast been in our distress;
A shelter from the storm thy wings afford,
   A succour from the tempest's furious stress,
   A rock's cool shade in the parched wilderness ;
Thro' everlasting ages still the same,
The Eternal, Great " I Am " thy changeless name !

Before her travail pangs befell the earth,
   Or nature, labouring in convulsions sore,
Brought the strong mountains forth, that monstrous
      birth,—
   Ere ocean poured her round each rising shore,
   Trembling beneath the shock and billowy roar,—
Thou reign'dst alone, in undisturbéd sway,
The same now, and for aye, as in the yesterday.

THE ETERNAL REFUGE.

Thou sitt'st supreme above the works of time,
    Immutable in thy eternity,
Over all chance and change enthroned sublime
    In unapproachéd might and majesty;
    Caprice, fate, circumstance, affect not thee:
Thou keep'st in perfect peace, and undismayed,
Whose minds are upon thee—the Rock of Ages—
    stayed.

Their refuge and abode the Eternal God—
    Beneath them stretch the everlasting arms,
So the fond mother-bird spreads wide abroad
    Her wings, and shields her brood from rude alarms,
    From day's swift peril, and dread nightly harms;
Though thousands fall around on every hand,—
Sustained by strength divine, fearless, unmoved
    they stand.

Built on the immutable, unshaken rock,
    Whose roots stand deep-fixed in eternity,—
They feel nor fear the superficial shock
    From which the births of time are seldom free;
    When winds and waves beat fierce and vehemently
'Gainst the frail structures founded on the sand,
Their utmost violence and fury *they* withstand.

THE ETERNAL REFUGE.

The changes we—weak timorous mortals—dread,
   O'er-whelming, rude, world-wide catastrophies,
When shakes the huge, firm earth on which we tread,
   And mountains plunge into the abyss of seas,—
   The pangs and fears the peoples' hearts that seize,
When into sore confusion all is hurled,—
They feel to be birth-pains of a better, fairer world.

Man in these changes doth participate :
   Mortal, and frail, fashioned from crude, mean clay—
He bides not, but removes from state to state ;
   Continuing never in one fixéd stay
   Doth the stern law of creaturehood obey ;
Ever to ruin and destruction turned,
As tho' the wrath divine against him fiercely burned.

This wrath is love's strange jealous energy,
   Stronger than death, more cruel than the grave,—
Eager from sin's fell grasp the soul to free,
   Thro' fiery judgments the true self to save,
   From gross and fleshly filthiness to lave ;
Love hath her coals of fire, her vehement flame,
Which viewed thro' fleshly film we ignorantly mis-
     name.

She leads man up from this world's wilderness
    'Mid blood, and fire, and pillars of thick smoke ;
Thro' stormy dawn—dark, doomful, pitiless,
    The day of God for man hath ever broke,
    The loud, deep trump his slumber hath awoke ;—
Then all our past but mere illusion seems,
Surprised we start from vain, false, visionary dreams.

All flesh appears frail as the perishing grass,
    That flourishes for one brief transient hour,—
Whose bloom into decay doth quickly pass,
    Soon spent the splendour of its floral dower
    Beneath fierce noon-day's torrid, fiery power ;
At morn in radiant beauty it appeared,—
  The eve beholds its pride — scorched, blasted,
    withered, seared :

So all man's beauty, grace, and comeliness
    Fades in the presence of thy glorious light,
Vile dust and ashes we ourselves confess—
    Placed in the focus of thy piercing sight ;
    Upon our fairest hopes falls foulest blight,—
When our misdeeds are set in thy full glance,
Our secret sins before thine awful countenance.

THE ETERNAL REFUGE.

The most felicitous and favoured life
   Seems but one long continued vanity,
With disappointment and vexation rife,—
   Our three-score years and ten fond misery;
   Our added days from labour sore scarce free;
Life appears tedious as a thrice-told tale,
Its interests, aims, and hopes, its pleasures wholly
   fail.

II.

O make us wise that we may understand
　Thy purpose herein, and thy high design!
May trace the wisdom that directs thy hand,
　Discern the workmanship of love divine;
　Upon our ignorance and blindness shine!
And show us how, 'mid ruin and decay,
The new world's fast foundations firmly thou dost
　　lay!

Grant us to see—behind the cloudy screen
　Close veils thy working from the vulgar eye,
What thine impenetrable counsels mean,
　Thy thoughts for our perception all too high!
　Into thy secret things we would not pry—
The mystic volume that is seven-sealed—
We seek alone what may to mortals be revealed,—

THE ETERNAL REFUGE.

The inchoate beauty—even now being wrought
  'Midst this chaotic scene of grief and pain,
The strange unearthly colouring oft-times caught
  By clouds surcharged with tempest, fire, and rain ;
  The growth that springs from life's sore stress and strain ;
How—amid anguish and disquietude,
The inward man with strength is secretly renewed ;—

Assured life's sharpest and most desperate grief
  Is light and momentary—when compared
With the pure joy surpassing man's belief,
  The rapturous bliss unspeakable prepared
  For those, who, as thro' life they patient fared,
Meekness, and truth, and righteousness have sought,
Waiting to see what love and power divine hath wrought ;—

Knowing by inward, clear, sure consciousness,
  Thy spirit bearing witness with our own,
That, —'mid the scathes that wreck, the woes oppress
  This earthly house, and cause the frequent moan,
  The shocks by which our hopes are overthrown,—
Some nobler form is coming to the birth,
That with some holy thing labours the travailing earth,— .

THE ETERNAL REFUGE.

Some fabric all divine, made not with hands,
   Nor sharing in the common frailty—
The imperfection that for ever brands
   Man's best performance with infirmity,
   A throne and temple for divinity,—
Where aye abides the presence of the Lord,
A shrine where his great name is worthily adored.

Impress with power upon us that this life
   Is to the life eterne the steep straight way,—
A bud to break in bloom—with beauty rife
   And fragrance ne'er dissolves nor fades away,
   The stormy dawn that ushers in fair day;—
Life's porch; the vestibule where souls eschew
Their garments flesh-defiled, and robes of light
      indue;—

Mere scaffolding of temporary use,
   And platform for the heavenly builder's feet,—
Swaying with every breath—till shaken loose,
   Blown to all winds, defunct, and obsolete;
   Shattered to dust—the fabric now complete;—
Veiling no longer from our darksome eyne
The glorious architect's sublimely grand design.

III.

GRANT that the feverish vicissitude
  Here mocks our hopes of settled rest and peace,
Affliction's frequent shocks severe and rude,
  From which is won nor respite, nor release,
  Pleasure's uncertain and precarious lease,—
May from earth's guileful snares our spirits free,
And toss our tortured souls on thy eternity!

Grant the bright heavenly vision that transcends
  The births of time, mounts its vexed troubled
    stream—
Earth-soiled as thro' these tracts terrene it wends—
  Gains the pure fount where living waters gleam,
  Escapes the tyranny of things that seem,
The illusion of these cheap, vain, garish shows,
The torment of unreal, imaginary woes!

THE ETERNAL REFUGE.

In the great purpose nearest to thine heart
  O make us eagerly co-operate ;
Act out on life's brief stage our proper part,
    Assist in hastening on the blesséd state
    Of earth and heavens sin-purged and new-create ;
No self-absorbed spectators let us stand
Of the marvels brought to pass by thine Almighty
    hand !

Thou art the potter, we the plastic clay,—
  Fashion and shape us after thine own will ;
Break up our hardness, in the mortar bray
    Our stubborn pride, thy mind in us fulfil ;
    Mould us each one a fitting utensil,
An honoured vessel for the Master's board,
With superscription graved, "Holiness to the
    Lord !"

O look upon the labour of our hands,
  And bless our purposes for they are thine !
We seek but to accomplish thy commands,
    To enter into thy sublime design ;
    Let the fair beauty of the Lord forth-shine,–
That inner glory—secretly being wrought
Thro' light affliction, — past all utterance, all
    thought !

THE ETERNAL REFUGE.

Let some faint gleam thereof at length be seen,
    Ere closes life's long, dark, tempestuous day!
Like as on evening clouds the golden sheen
    Shot from the sinking sun's last farewell ray,
    When on their scattering ranks the light-shafts
        play;
Now in our eventide let there be light,
Ere on us there descend the shades of mortal night!

Comfort us now after the tedious years
    Wherein thy afflicting hand on us hath lain!
Return to those, who long have sown in tears
    Soil-harrowed by the cruel rack of pain!
    Quicken to life the grief-bedewéd grain!
Smile thou upon us,—in that smile is spring,
So shall our desolate hearts henceforth exult and
    sing!

BEFORE THE BATTLE.

Ps. xx.

BEFORE THE BATTLE.

In the day of thy distress,
When the foemen sorely press,
And their threatening front display—
Marshalled in fierce proud array,
Let the God of Jacob hear,
Jahveh to thy prayer give ear!

Help thee from the sanctuary,
Out of Zion strengthen thee!
From his awful cloudy seat,
The dark thunder's close retreat,
Home of the consuming flame,
Manifest his holy name!

Thence the volleying levin gleams
In swift, livid, torrent streams!
There the fiery tokens see
Of his angered jealousy,—
Eager to protect and save
Who his care and succour crave!

In thy day of trouble bring
Thine appropriate offering!
Freely tender all thy heart,
With thy fondest idols part—
All that's dearest in thine eyes,
Bind with cords the sacrifice!

Lust from out thy being stamp,
Cast that Achan from the camp!
All the blood of self-hood spill,
Make thine own the supreme will!
Purge thee from the leaven of pride,
Let no lurking evil hide!

These Jehovah cannot brook,
Unto this man doth he look—
Contrite, and in spirit poor,
With the pure he shows him pure;
Men of haughty looks and high
He beholds with distant eye.

He will all thy hopes fulfil
When thou makest thine His will,—
Hearts instinct with heavenly fire
See accomplished their desire;
Armoured in celestial light
Thou shalt vanquish in the fight.

Lo the sacred levin rends
Heaven's high vault, and swift descends!
On the proffered sacrifice
Falls acceptance from the skies!
Savour of a smell most sweet
Riseth to the mercy seat!

Freely mounts the heart's true prayer,
Climbs the gracious golden stair,
Entereth the inmost shrine,
Where the ministers divine
In the heavenly presence stand,
Waiting the divine command!

Thence like flashing flames they speed
Help to bring thee in thy need;
Put no trust in fleshly force,
Chariot or battle horse,—
Wait upon Jehovah,—He
Gives alone the victory!

Now know I the Lord is nigh
To the saint's distressful cry,
Thro' wide earth 'twill yet be known
Jahveh careth for his own;
Succour in their need is given—
Holpen from the highest heaven.

BEFORE THE BATTLE.

The salvation Thou hast sought,
Seasonably for thee wrought,
We thy followers shall share,
Strong through thee to do and dare;
Victory by thee secured
For all Israel is assured.

We too our free-gift will bring,
Blend it with thine offering,
By thy high example fired,
With a kindred hope inspired;
In thy name our foes defy,
Lift the drooping banner high!

Victory our banners crown,
They are fallen and cast down!
From the east nor from the west
Comes promotion, 'tis confest;
Jahveh, supreme over all,
Hearkeneth his people's call.

TRANSFIGURATION THROUGH SUFFERING.

1 PETER III. 18-20.

TRANSFIGURATION THROUGH SUFFERING.

The flesh to death abandoned,—liberty
And life abundant are the spirit's fee,
She now obtains her due supremacy;

Her forfeited inheritance regains,
Enters upon her rightful, fair domains,
Thro' the strait difficult gate of travail pains;

Escapes for ever sin's enslaving mesh—
Close woven by the witchery of flesh,
In heaven's pure life-fount bathes herself afresh.

Ardent she presses upward still and nigher
The blest celestial presence, with the choir
Seraphic to unite—her sole desire.

* * * * * *

Even He the just, who for unjust men died,
His spirit felt with quickening power supplied
As from his veins fast ebbed life's purple tide.

His spiritual forces were matured
Through the deep pain and anguish he endured,
Over all flesh full power he thus procured:

In that new might thro' death's dark realms he sped,
With the glad gospel for the imprisoned dead,
For bowed-down souls uplifting of the head.

His way thro' all obstructing foes he fought,
For universal man deliverance wrought,
Not for the quick alone,—his victory bought

Freedom for whom dark Sheol's bonds detain,
Spirits in that drear prison long had lain,—
Unhumbled, and unbroke—they spurned his reign;

Refused the fiery baptism of pain,
Chose the unhallowed, lawless way of Cain,
Immersed in pleasure, ease, and greed of gain.

They entered not the ark with the righteous few,
What time the heavens their dreadful curtain drew,
And the wild deluge swept the world from view;—

But o'er them the all-whelming waters past,—
Who wrath against the day of wrath amassed,
From the fair rainbow-circled earth outcast.

*　　*　　*　　*　　*　　*

The covering now is rent, the mean disguise
Still veils his glory from dim flesh-filmed eyes;
Spirits adore whom mortal men despise:

Erst disobedient souls rebel no more,
Awed by that visage marred; those marks of
  gore,
That tell of the stupendous pains he bore.

II.

ALIKE for saved men—as for him who saves—
Avail the fiery baptismal waves,
The path to blessing tribulation paves.

Witness the malefactor at Christ's side
Proffering kingly homage ere he died,
Abjured his scornful rage, his rebel pride.

Thro' the rent flesh, by sharpest anguish torn,
Breaks the glad dawn of fair redemption's morn,
Into Christ's kingdom a blest babe is born :

Now lives the spirit as the flesh decays,
The gibe of blasphemy is changed to praise,
On his late-found prince and chief bent his rapt
 gaze.

Himself already numbered with the dead—
Of death-doomed men in Christ he sees the head,
Deep in his breast bright new-create hopes are
 bred.

His lips e'en now tasting death's bitter wave—
His monarch greets this man in guise of slave,
Sees glory's pathway issue from the grave ;—

In shame and suffering finds kingly worth,
Basis of empire shareth not with earth,—
But from the abyss of anguish springs to birth.

The secret from his people kept he knows,—
Death, insult, torture are no real woes,
Nor Greek, nor Roman, Israel's deadliest foes;

And in his new-born faith ecstatic cries,—
" Remember me when king!"—his king replies:
" To-day thou'lt be with me in Paradise."

With the meek submissive flock the Shepherd feeds
By living waters, and thro' fruitful meads,
He finds full-satisfied his wakened needs.

Thus must He yet appear to all the race
In unveiled majesty, before his face
Of awful love sin's hardness melts apace.

* * * * * *

'Tis suffering crowns the brow with aureole,
Imprints imperial features on the soul,
Empowers frail, feeble man to play the kingly role.

THE REDEEMED CITY.

Ps. XLVI. to XLVIII.

THE REDEEMED CITY.

I.

God is a refuge sure and strong,
   Ever at hand to help and save ;
E'en when he seems to tarry long,
   And round his ark the tempests rave,—
He reckoneth up his people's tears,
With the first dawn his aid appears.

Tho' the light mountains leap and skip
   In wild delirious revelry,
And their imperious summits dip
   Deep in the unplumbed central sea ;
While the pale terror-stricken shore
Shudders at ocean's maddening roar,—

THE REDEEMED CITY.

Fearless we rest amidst the rage,
    The shock of the resistless storm,
Tho' the fierce war the elements wage
    The face of continents deform;
Fearless we rest and undismayed,
High o'er the storm our hopes are laid.

Founded upon the whelming seas,
    On the wild flood establishéd,
Home of tranquility and ease,
    With living streams celestial fed,
By the fell foeman's foot untrod
Unmoved remains the Mount of God,—

The heavenly Jerusalem,
    Where with his saints Jehovah dwells;
Nor violence nor stratagem
    Prevails against her citadels;
Her habitants abide secure,
Their bread dealt free, their waters sure.

THE REDEEMED CITY.

Munitions of protecting rocks
    Encircle her on every side,
The steep, sheer, crystal rampart mocks
    The angry powers 'gainst her allied;
A wall of fire engirds her round,
Within—'tis peaceful holy ground.

Jahveh himself shall be to her
    A generous, large, full-brimming stream,
On whose still breast no pillager
    Guides the black brazen-beaked trireme;
Galley with bulwarks towering high
Nor gallant bark shall pass thereby.

II.

Breaks the impetuous eastern gale
  On ships of Tarshish in their pride,
In vain they spread the bursting sail,
  Idly the oarsman's art is plied;
In vain they stay the tottering mast,
The tacklings yield before the blast:

See! where the meeting tides conflict,
  'Mid the loud billows' wild turmoil,
The ill-starred, shattered derelict
  Heaps on the shore the scattered spoil!
Rich is the harvest of the sand,
The gathered gains of many a land.

THE REDEEMED CITY.

Broke is the bow! and snapped the spear!
   The chariot given to the flame,
Blood-crimsoned garb, and foeman's gear!
   The men of might are put to shame!
Strong stupor, deep perpetual sleep,
Earth's heroes in oblivion steep!

For, in the morning watch, the Lord
   Looked from his tabernacling cloud;
Remembering his plighted word—
   Like a roused lion cried aloud
Upon his foes,—smit with dismay
Melted the foeman's might away.

III.

Like tempest-stricken mountain peak,
  Emerging from the night of storm—
Ruin thereon had sought to wreak,
  And all its majesty deform;
The clinging folds of lingering mist
Are with the morning's splendour kissed.

Nature's kind healing hand inwreathes
  With strange new grace the landscape lone,
On the bleak desolate scene she breathes
  A beauty all before unknown,—
Jealous the injury to repair
Inflicted on her features fair.

THE REDEEMED CITY.

So from night's gloom and mantling cloud
    Shines forth the new Jerusalem,—
Off-flinging her dark murksome shroud,—
    A royal, sparkling diadem,
A jewelled crown in Jahveh's hands
Forth to the wondering world she stands,—

Fair as the clear, unclouded moon
    Whole-orbed! bright as the blazing sun
Riding in high meridian noon,
    Joying his arduous course to run!
Terrible, as in the battle day
A bannered host in full array!

Her light has come, the light of God
    Has risen on her obscurity;
Conspicuous it beams abroad
    For furthest ends of earth to see,—
Whom shades of darkness still oppress,
The prey of bitter, sharp distress.

All that her beauty sought to dim
    Contributes to enhance her joy,
Swells the full choral triumph hymn,
    Her ransomed people's grave employ;
Gladness is given her for distress,
Garments of praise for heaviness.

" The day hath dawned, arise and shine!"
    She hears the all-creative voice,
Wakes from her lethargy supine,
    Obeys the blest command, " Rejoice!"
The dust and ash from off her shakes,
As the bright morn upon her breaks.

IV.

Shame-smitten earth's proud kings pass by
  Struck dumb with deep astonishment,
Gazing askance with sidling eye,
  These things to alter impotent,—
For to the Lord belong the shields
Of earth, the power supreme he wields.

Our adversaries are afraid,
  Confounded at these dread portents;
On the pale lip the hand they lay,
  Silent and deep in their laments;
As serpents in the dust that creep,
As worms from out their holes that peep.

THE REDEEMED CITY.

The hill of Zion hath become
    The joy of the wide-peopled earth,
Of myriad tribes the acknowledged home,
    Jubilant with high holy mirth;
All nations come to worship there,
Their chosen, hallowed shrine of prayer.

Around her bulwarks and her walls
    We walk, mark well the embattled towers,
Explore her palaces and halls
    Thro' days of peace and tranquil hours;
These marvellous events we spell
Latest posterity to tell.

Like as we've heard we now have seen
    In the blest city of our God;
The sights that greet our dazzled een
    Transcend the fame has gone abroad;
Past griefs from memory they blot, -
The former troubles are forgot.

Calmly the past we meditate,
  How idly puerile appear
The apprehensions that so late
  Filled our weak hearts with coward fear!
The terrors that so great had grown
'Mid night's thick gloom with morn are flown

Where is the militant array
  Late lay encamped around our home,
Inspiring such profound dismay
  None from his place would dare to roam?
Where—who about our ramparts hung,
The people of strange barbarous tongue?

V.

How were my inmost bowels stirred,
  When, pealing harshly from afar,
The trump's deep piercing blast was heard,
  And all the dread alarm of war!
Visions of horror uncontrolled
In crowding billows o'er me rolled.

I looked, and lo! the earth was waste,
  The heavens all desolate of light!
The mountains shook and fled in haste,
  The hills had vanished from the sight!
Of man and beast the land was lone,
The affrighted fowls far off were flown!

THE REDEEMED CITY.

From the frontier of distant Dan
   Is heard the snorting of his steeds!
As the foe's swift-advancing van
   On vengeful task of judgment speeds;
Hark! the destroyer on his way,
The ravening lion scents the prey.

E'en as a land the Lord doth bless,
   Dear object of his care, earth smiled
Before them,—a bleak wilderness,
   Down-trampled, blasted, and defiled,
As where had waged some deadly fray,
Marked the fell desolater's sway!

How trembled we from hour to hour,
   As breathless hurried in the posts
With tidings of the invader's power
   Pressing unhindered thro' our coasts!
With pale, fear-stricken countenance
We followed his blood-tracked advance:—

Here they laid up their carriages,
  They lodged at Geba for this night
Now they are past the passages,
  And Gibeah has ta'en to flight!
Gallim lifts up a cry of fear,
Which Anathoth and Laish hear!

Well we remember that dread day
  On the hill of Nob he took his stand,
Marshall'd war's terrible array,
  And shook contemptuously his hand
Against our bulwarks many-towered,
'Neath which like timorous sheep we cowered.

As some wide-spreading vigorous tree
  Lifts high its head in leafy pride,
Of goodly growth and fair to see,
  Well planted by the river side,—
That under its usurping boughs
Rival or neighbour none allows ;—

Thus their deep darkening shade they flung
   O'er Jesse's shorn, truncated stem,
When on the mount their banners hung
   Over against Jerusalem;
As tho' to rob of light and air
The nursling of Jehovah's care;—

Till—roused to jealousy—he lops
    The huge, proud, earth - o'ershadowing
      bough;
The arm uplifted powerless drops,
    Jesse's poor stem may flourish now—
Of the broad forest fairest crown,
A plant of large world-wide renown.

VI.

Silenced the sneer, the taunting gibe,
  The bitter boast of blasphemy!
Where now the learn'd, the busy scribe,
  His craft and frustrate industry?
The vaunting utterances he wrote
None ventures now against us quote.

Their braggart voice they lifted high
  In scurrilous, blaspheming tone;
The living God they durst defy,
  Assailed with scorn the heavenly throne;
Dared to compare with the Supreme
The figments of their baseless dream:—

THE REDEEMED CITY.

" Shall we not, as we dealt with them
    Whose hope was placed in other gods,
So deal with this Jerusalem,
    This Jahveh she so loudly lauds
What god is there of any land
Hath saved his servants from our hand ? '

Boast ye no more, nor vainly mock,
    Abate your arrogance and pride !
Their Rock was not as our Rock,
    His people's hope who ne'er belied
Our enemies themselves report
No god can save in such a sort.

The daughter of Jerusalem
    Thy boastful utterance treats with scorn ;
Whom insolently dost thou contemn ?
    'Gainst whom exaltest high the horn ?
The Holy One of Israel—
Between the Cherubim doth dwell !

As if the axe should vainly vaunt
    Against the hand therewith that hews;
The rod with impotency taunt
    The arm its ministry should use:
Jahveh's strange judgment-work complete,
Its instruments are obsolete.

VII.

Our loss retrieved, we take the prey,
    Seize on the late recovered spoil;
On our just fief the hand we lay,
    Win back the fruits of our own toil;
Now that hath ceased the spoiler's rage,
Re-enter on our heritage.

THE REDEEMED CITY.

From Dan to Beersheba the land
   To us is subjugate again;
The Lord hath issued His command,—
   Her desolate highways flow with men;
Manasseh and far Gilead
Avouch Jerusalem their head.

Shechem and Succoth's fruitful vale
   Are measured out for us by line;
Judah their law-giver all hail,
   Moab! the menial's task is thine;
Our banners o'er Philistia flew,
On Edom we cast out the shoe.

The stranger's soil—far as the eye
   Can range—hath fallen to our lot;
At our dispose its treasures lie,
   The wells deep digg'd that we digg'd not;
Vineyards unplanted by our hand,
Homes ready-built, at our command.

Henceforth we number as our friends
   Rahab and haughty Babylon ;
E'en to the earth's remotest ends
   The nations' hearts are fixed upon
Israel as their true father-land,
Where'er hoar ocean laves the strand.

The oppressor of the earth hath ceased,
   Who smote the peoples with his rod ;
From spoilure are the lands released
   By the despot's iron feet down-trod
Who made the world a wilderness
Hath none to pity his distress.

The earth is quiet and at rest,
   She breaketh forth in voice of song,—
Since none surviveth to molest,
   None breathes to do her scathe or wrong ;
The forest claps its hands for glee
Since from the feller's axe set free.

VIII.

For thee! thy fame is but a breath,
   A wind that passeth swift away;
A shameful, ignominious death
   Waits thy inglorious outcast clay;
In vain thou seekest to secure
The customed rights of sepulture!

In vain thou seek'st a burial-place
   Amongst the honourable dead;
With men of pure, high-lineaged race
   Would'st rest in peace thy perjured head!
Hades' dark crypt they scorn to share,
Challenge thy right of entry there.

Thou who did'st erst thyself account
   A god, and like to the Most High;
Would'st sit upon the holy mount,
   Erect thy throne above the sky;—
Thy pomp is levelled with the grave,
The worm consumes thy beauty brave.

Sheol at thy approach doth wake,
   She summoneth her shades to see
The conqueror wide earth did shake,—
   They look upon thee narrowly;
They ask—" Art thou too fallen thus,
Art thou become like unto us?"

IX.

Our Priest-king doth no longer stand
 Clothed in habiliments of shame,
Our mortal foe at his right hand
 With strong irrefutable claim ;
Full expiation hath been made,
Our debt e'en to the double paid !

In his full beauty he appears,
 Benign, majestically meek ;
No longer the defacing tears
 Stream frequent down his channelled cheek ;
From his dimmed eyes strange joy hath
  gleamed,—
It is the year of his redeemed !

In our prolonged affliction he
   Felt the affliction as his own,
Touched with profoundest sympathy,
   Flesh of our flesh, bone of our bone;
Our sorrow *his*, our sore annoy,
His the rejoicing in our joy.

'Twas our reproach that broke his heart
   When came the foe against our wall,
And hurled the flaming fiery dart—
   Words steeped in wormwood and in gall;
The taunts against us freely flung
His gentle soul with anguish wrung.

Our day of trouble and rebuke
   Was that to him of bitterest woe;
Since our infirmities he took
   His cup was filled to overflow;
Sore stricken was he for our wound,
So finely was his spirit tuned.

Our chastisement on him was laid,
    For our transgressions he was bruised,
For us the scapegoat he was made
    Since for our guilt he stood accused;—
His wounds remedial balsam yield,
His people by his stripes are healed.

In sackcloth clad, foul ashes shed
    Upon his consecrated brow,
In the vile dust his kingly head
    In meek abasement he did bow;
And called, with strong outcries and tears,
On him who saved him from his fears.

X.

The spectacle of his great grief
   Woke our insensibility,
In bitter tears we found relief,
   And wept with him in sympathy,—
To sorrow and contrition brought
As by contagion from him caught.

The holy unction on him shed
   In gracious shower—our souls imbues,
As the oil on Aaron's sacred head
   Flowed to his furthest skirt, as dews
Falling on Hermon's heights distill
Their balmy sweets on Zion's hill.

We look upon the wounded one,
   With anguish and compunction torn,
As for a loved and only son,
   Alone, apart, we sit and mourn,—
Till opes a cleansing fount divine,
Whose waters with our tears combine.

From sin's alloy and dross now purged,
   Regained our prime, our best estate,
Wiped out the charge against us urged—
   Rebellious city designate,—
Transformed are we, create anew,
And named Jehovah-Tzidkenu.

Sick from foot-sole to crown of head,
   And to the innermost heart-core;
With the blood of her defilement red,
   One universal fluent sore;—
Behold her now from sickness free,
Forgiven her foul iniquity!

XI.

Henceforth, O Lord! thy glorious Name
    We will exalt, thy praises speak;
Of all thou'st wrought spread wide the fame,
    Who rightest the oppressed and weak;
All things are present to thy thought,
Thy counsels with deep wisdom fraught.

Earth's fencéd cities are a heap,
    O'erthrown the Babels of the world;
Perished the impregnably strong keep,
    Into sheer hopeless ruin hurled;
Those cities ne'er shall be rebuilt
Wherein thy servants' blood was spilt!

Thou wast a refuge for the poor
   And needy—in their sore distress,
Bulwark and shelter strong and sure
   'Gainst the wild raging tempest's stress;
A shadow from the burning heat
When fierce the blasting noon-beams beat!

THE DISCIPLINE OF PAIN.

HEB. XII. 1 to 13.

THE DISCIPLINE OF PAIN.

I.

Despise not thou the chastening of the Lord,
Nor weary of his strong rebuking word ;
Strive not the healthful flow of grief to stay,
Nor prematurely for deliverance pray.

Reckon thy pain no purposeless, vain thing,
But as the precious stone on life's dull ring ;
Treasure its moments with a miser's care,
Thou yet may'st deem them all too few and rare ;—

When standing on the brink of heaven's far shore
May'st wish thee back on earth to suffer more—
Once tasted the fair, blest, ambrosial fruit,
Brought forth from grief's unpalatable root,—

And sore regret—if there regrets could be
Where thy will's blent with God's eternally—
Thy chance of winning has now passed for aye
The pearls in sorrow's sunless depths that lay.

Thy sorrow as a crown thou then shalt wear,
Clasp to thy close embrace the irksome care;
Each tear-drop shall transmute to some rich gem
Thou'dst miss from thy consummate diadem.

When flesh is pierced with sorrow's sharpest pang,—
'Tis to prepare a place wherein to hang
The jewels wherewith they are beautified,
Who share the honours of the slain Lamb's Bride.

II.

Faint not e'en when thy torment grows intense,—
This momentary grief means gain immense;—
When fiercest flames the furnace,—then most sure
And full the metal's flow, dross-cleansed and pure.

Fear not!—who giveth power to the faint
With thy great weariness is well acquaint;
'Tis when our youthful vigour wholly fails,
The strength divine for succour most avails.

He maketh sore, then binds the broken heart;
Wounds to display his wondrous healing art:
Puts to his people's lips the bitter bowl,
Whose sovereign virtues renovate the soul.

Regard not chastisement as penalty,
Cure rather of sin's baleful malady;—
Pleasure's drugged fulsome cup for dregs contains
Medicinal and salutary pains.

All forms of suffering generate at length
A dormant energy and latent strength;
Some strange remedial force still underlies
The most o'er-whelming of calamities.

The change that ends illusive happiness,
And frees us from the world's too-fond caress,—
Proves the true mystic talisman to ope
Vistas of joy transcending utmost hope.

Is thine through life the weeping, melting mood,
With frequent-starting tears thine eyes bedewed?—
Grief's film-detergent, purifying flow
Of regions far clear vision shall bestow.

III.

All chastening for the present grievous seems,—
Its gracious purpose the chastised mis-deems ;
Not while fierce wintry storms lay waste the ground—
Fair laughing flowers and fragrant fruits are found :—

While still the darkened welkin thunders loud—
Thy spirit wrapt in thickest earth-born shroud—
The bright light in the cloud remains unseen,
All veiled its inner-lining's silvery sheen.

Who goeth forth beneath cold weeping skies,
And life's wild rude inclemency defies—
Sowing in patience and assured belief,—
Well laden comes with rich, ripe, golden sheaf.

They who through tedious years were plagued full
    sore,
Whom suffering's long continued stress outwore,—
On them the beauty of the Lord shall shine,
Made manifest thro' weakness and decline;—

In them the workmanship divine shall be
Shown, for their children yet unborn to see
How Heaven from ruin and decay can raise
Materials for millenniums of praise.

IV.

Lift up the hands that hang, the unhinged knees!
Keep the straight path! lest when thy brother sees
Thee halt or turn aside,—the strong! the bold!—
On virtue he relax his feeble hold.

Consider Him who trod life's dreary road,
Bearing for thee sin's dread stupendous load,—
By vision of the distant and unseen
Up-borne, despised things present and terrene;—

Prince-leader of the faithful martyr band,
To whom this earth was a dry barren land;
Who, finding here no true congenial home,
Looked for the abiding city yet to come.

Encompassed by their cloudy legion host,
Henceforth be this alone thy pride and boast,—
That to thee—all-unworthy—has been given,
With firstborn souls a place and name in heaven.

V.

If thou endure with patience,—as a son
God deals with thee; assure thee that not one
True child the rod of discipline escapes,
In some one form of pain's oft shifting shapes.

To be from chastisement exempt would prove
Goodness unwisely kind, defective love:—
By keenest anguish, pain's most poignant smart,
Thy interest thou mayest gauge in Love's great heart.

Let sorrow be the royal seal and sign
Proclaims thee sprung from parentage divine;
The greatness of thy sufferings presage
The glory of the promised heritage.

VI.

The fathers of our flesh, our worldly weal
Consulting, spared us not—preferred to steel
Their hearts against our passionate outcries,
Flesh to its higher ends to sacrifice.

Obsequious reverence to them we paid,
Unquestioning their every wish obeyed,—
For nobler ends let us obedience give,
Accept the birth-pains by which spirits live.

Too often their corrections, through caprice,
The faults they sought to cure served but to
    increase—
No stroke the All-wise God in love inflicts
The highest, wisest purpose contradicts:

No low ignoble aim he contemplates,
But flesh to spirit's claims subordinates,—
The Father of our spirits—his chief care
That in the blest, eternal life they share ;—

That—freed from the entanglement of flesh—
Its subtle, intricate, close-woven mesh—
Like birds escaped the fowler's broken snare,
We soar to breathe the clear celestial air ;—

That—to the claims of flesh thro' suffering dead—
We drink, at love's pure living fountain-head,
The love divine into our inmost heart,
Love which alone true sonship can impart.

Lord ! who art light,—since fellowship with thee
Implies a soul emancipate and free
From fleshly thrall,—O grant us to possess
Participation in thy holiness ;

By chastisement the power of darkness smite,
Meetness bestow,—to share with saints in light
The kingdom of thy well belovèd son;
For this high end no shame no sacrifice we shun.

IN EXITU ISRAEL.

Ps. CXIV.

IN EXITU ISRAEL.

When from the house of our bondage we came
The Lord went before us in pillar of flame;
Judah was then for Jehovah the shrine,
Israel felt the afflatus divine.

Backward astonished the startled waves flew,
Full-flowing Jordan his waters withdrew;
Leaped the huge mountains like high-bounding rams,
Skipped, as in terror, the hills like young lambs.

Whence this dismay, thou disquieted sea,
Proud-swelling Jordan, why tim'rously flee?
Why quake ye thus, ye strong mountains and hills,
Whence is this panic creation that fills?

IN EXITU ISRAEL.

Earth trembles sore at the presence of God,
Over all nature is stretched forth his rod,—
Turning the rock into clear living streams,
Wonders performing surpassing our dreams.

Still is it with the Lord's Israel so,
Forth from sin's slavery whene'er they go;
Still is there heard as the shout of a king,
When earth's vile shackles from off them they fling.

The earth is deep moved; to the heart of the sea
The mountains down-hurled; the little hills flee;
When thou goest forth for thy people, O God!
Thro' the dread wilderness making a road.

Day's bright blazing orb is eclipsed at high noon,
To sackcloth it turneth, to blood the pale moon,
When the Lord's notable, terrible day
Breaks, that forbids us in slumber delay.

Then we awake from sin's perilous sleep,
With the Lórd's Israël our passover keep ;
Freely ourselves as his people avow,
His will obeying whereto all things bow.

All things are possible for Israél,
Vanquished the forces of death and of hell !
Faith's potent rod in the babe's feeble hand
Victory winneth o'er ocean and land.

All that thy heavenward course would impede
Must be removed in the day of thy need ;
Comes the temptation in whatsoe'er shape
Straight is provided a way of escape.

When thro' the fire thou passest—the flame
Plays round thee harmless, impotent, tame ;
Though thro' deep waters thy pathway shall lie,
All their proud fury thy faith shall defy.

Surely 'gainst Israel enchantment is not,
Vain the diviner's contrivance and plot!
No weapon—fashioned with purpose to kill—
Prospers apart from the heavenly will.

All things submit to Jehovah's control,
Vainly the war-smith enkindleth the coal!
Vainly the waster essays to destroy,
Blunted each tool he would 'gainst thee employ!

Fear not the arrow that flieth by day!
No nightly plague let thy spirit dismay!
Object of care to the Great King of kings—
Round thee are folded his covering wings.

From the fierce glare of the burning noontide
God's tabernacle a shade will provide,
'Mid the thick gloom of the sable-hued night
The fiéry pillar shall furnish thee light.

Askest thou, " how should Jehovah prepare
Bread in the wilderness, naked and bare ? "
Manna shall drop round thy tents like the dew,
Food for thy hunger surprising and new.

Rageth thy thirst unendurably sore ?—
Rivers abundant their streams shall outpour,
Source most unlooked for refreshment shall bring,
From the hard rock living fountains upspring.

Jahveh the sword of thy excellency—
Helper and Shield ! Who is like unto thee—
Favoured of Heaven, O blest Israél !
Aloud and afar his high praises forth-tell !

A PEOPLE FOR HIS PRAISE.

Ps. LXVI. and LXVII.

A PEOPLE FOR HIS PRAISE.

Sing to the Lord, with voice of mirth,
Break forth in song, O silent earth!
    And bless his sacred name;
Say unto God, " How great art thou!
Thine enemies before thee bow,
    And kiss the dust for shame."

Sublimely throned Jehovah rules,
Forbear, ye proud rebellious fools,
    On high to uprear the horn;
Rather with us your voice unite,
Proclaim his all-victorious might,
    To praise convert your scorn.

Come and behold the works of God,
Sustained by his strong arm we trod
 Dry-foot the threatening wave;
Into firm land he turns the main,
O'er earth and sea extends his reign,
 His chosen saints to save.

List, while we tell what he hath wrought,
The help to our sore need he brought,
 Numbered amongst the dead!
Our failing life how he restored,
New hopes into our spirits poured,
 Lifted on high our head.

With fear and anguish wild beset,
Entangled in affliction's net,
 Birds taken in the snare;
He broke for us the fowler's toil,
The spoiler robbed of his sure spoil,
 Responsive to our prayer.

A PEOPLE FOR HIS PRAISE.

Men rode in triumph o'er our head,
Deep waters o'er life's path were spread,
    We passed thro' flood and flame;
As silver from its vile dross tried,
In pain's fierce furnace purified,
    Thro' woe to wealth we came.

O, praise ye our prayer-hearing Lord!
Who hath despised not nor abhorred
    The poor man's mean estate,—
But bent Him to his feeble cry,
With tenderest regard drew nigh,
    Raised him and made him great.

'Tis fitting we His name should bless,
And vows pledged freely in distress
    Be cheerfully discharged;
Joyful and loud to praise 'tis meet
Who set at liberty our feet,
    Our narrow room enlarged.

When we shall publish wide abroad
The wonders our all-gracious God
    Wrought for our burdened souls;
His way through earth's bounds shall be known,
Mankind their idol gods disown,
    Fling them to bats and moles.

From the far climes of furthest earth,
Distrest by spiritual dearth,
    The perishing peoples come—
Crying: "Our father's hopes were lies,
Things profitless and vanities,
    To our entreaties dumb."

Henceforth from wars the peoples cease,
Earth yields her plentiful increase,
    Unstained her rivers glide;
Their spears they turn to pruning hooks,
Their swords to plough-shares; haughty looks
    And fierce they lay aside.

Exalted now in all men's eyes,
See Salem o'er the mountains rise!
    The nations thither flow;
" Come let us scale the sacred mount "
They cry, " where springs life's full free fount.
    We too will with you go."

EPICTETUS.

EPICTETUS.

    WHATEVER shall befall,
    Within, without, is all—
(So spake the Master, in mean guise of slave)
    Of " good and evil" blent,
    And " things indifferent ; "
His manly counsel take, and prove thee wise and brave!

    " Good " is a thing of mind,
    In so far as affined
Its temper to the true, the pure, the right ;
    " Evil "—the will all prone,
    Flung from its proper throne,
And mastership by force of passion's headstrong might.

Thine is the good or ill,
Which, cleaving to thee still,
Attests thy value in the scale divine;
The rest is but a loan,
Another's; not thine own;
That which for aye abides—that alone reckon thine.

Nought else of moment is—
As source of bane or bliss,
Things towards or from which eagerly men run!
Misnamed prosperity,
Sickness, loss, poverty,—
Let not the illusive show tempt thee to seek or shun;—

No vain appearance mock
Thy hopes, no terror shock
Thy high resolve; but 'neath the hollow mask
And show, what each new thing
Of good or ill can bring,
As fair or frowning form accosts thee, promptly ask.

'Tis not within thy power
To fix thy natal hour
Or place, to choose thine earthly destiny;
By circumstances bound,
Conditioned all around,
Best use to make of things—for this alone thou'rt free.

Poor toy for hours of mirth,
Of scant intrinsic worth,
The ball the players lightly toss at will;
All centres in the game,
Thence alone praise or blame
Accrues—proportioned to the player's strength and skill.

What luck the dies may bring,
When on the board they ring,
The gamester knows not, much less can command;
His—be it great or small
The number that shall fall—
With utmost skill to employ such chance as comes to hand.

What but mere balls and dies
All to the sealéd eyes
Of low-browed worldlings stands in most esteem?
Assigning thy reward—
Thy Master will regard
Not the theme given to treat, but how thou treat'st the theme.

It boots not whether placed
Low in life's scale, or graced
With all that beauty, wit, or wealth e'er gave;
In either case thy part
Calls for consummate art,
Treading time's stage in mask of king, swain, knight, or knave.

Man works in various stuff,
The delicate or rough,
Shaping the material to his taste or whim;
Thine be this task assigned,—
To mould aright the mind,
Her features fashion true, a perfect portrait limn.

Thy aim to concentrate
Give heed, avoid the fate
Dogs their uncertain steps who strive to keep
Two purposes in view,
The illusive and the true;
From such distracted toil but scant the gain they reap.

To this true end be leal,
If, hourly, things unreal
Seduce thee thence, thou'st missed life's one grand
aim :
Straight to the goal then hie,
Accomplish—ere thou die—
The supreme task for which the stern hours lay their
claim.

Bound for a distant shore,
Whence thou return'st no more,
Let no base lure of earth tempt thy fond stay;
If—gathering shells or weed—
The shipman call, make speed
To re-embark, and fling thy flotsam spoil away.

With wealth increases care
And irksome cark; they fare
The best whom fewest fretful wants disturb:
Who multiplies his needs
Troubles unnumbered breeds;
True affluence theirs alone unbridled lust who curb.

Thy pride and vanity
Provoke the enmity
Of minds, like thine, still deep immersed in self;
His splendour who displays
The self-same fault betrays,
Prompts the poor thief to steal, base thirst for earthly pelf.

Ne'er can true liberty
Be thine, until thou free
Thy soul from eager greed of grosser good;
Would'st humbly cringe and fawn?
To please the filthy spawn,
Hot luxury doth hatch, adapt thy changeful mood?

Most vulnerable they,
Their lives who subject lay,
By fond attachments, to rude fortune's blows;
Where best the stroke may tell
Of aim directed well,
Shielding his shrinking head, the snake instructs his foes.

Prepare thee to endure;
The hardship will inure
Thy powers, and thy yet lacking strength supply:
The painful exercise,
Exacting tears and cries,
Deprived thee, through disuse sterile thy virtues lie.

Reckon thou with the cost
Of being wise, nor boast
Untimely of the heights thou hop'st to reach:
Master thine own task well—
To others slow to tell
Thy lore, apt scholarship secure ere thou dost teach.

Let thy life speak for thee,
Than froth-spume of the sea
Lighter thy word, respondent not thy deed;
The law supreme enacts,—
The fruit of our own acts,
Our influence shall spread, wholesome or hurtful seed.

Who the Olympian prize
Aspire toward—despise
Inglorious ease and self-indulgent claims;
Using such abstinence
As thwarts thy grosser sense,
Let *thy* pains their's surpass, as loftier tend thine aims.

For nought we nothing win;
Think well ere thou begin
The task, if thou hast strength to carry through;
Lest men with mockery greet
Thy merited defeat,
And the presumption of thine enterprise thou rue.

Think not attainment cheap,
Nor hope, with instant leap,
Heights by heroic souls hard won to gain :—
Gradual the fruit matures,
Slow patient growth ensures
The fibre firm and close of the timber's well-knit grain.

The learner's strains strike harsh,
The first steps on the march
Of the upward slope are difficult and slow;
Ere long to discord's reign
Succeeds some dulcet strain;
That desperate steep once past thy path will smoother grow.

A different rule is found
For sickly men and sound;
The strong attempt what feebler folk forbear:
Wait, convalescent soul,
Thine invalid frame made whole—
The strife thou shunnest now undaunted then thou'lt dare.

Yet, while thy strength's still weak,
Its increase thou must seek
By exercise of that at thy command;
The skill the warrior learns
On lesser fields, he turns
To purpose when there dawns some morn of battle grand.

Hast thou received offence,
Unkindness, violence?
To reason eitherwise it rests with thee:—
Intolerable this wrong;
Or, they to me belong,
Brothers and kin of blood, who wrought the injury.

Would'st grace the board, and make
Things mean and vulgar take
A glorified aspéct, and statelier state?
The impatient thought restrain,
From angry heat refrain,
Grace with thy gentleness who on thy service wait.

Seated at life's full board,
Bear not thyself toward
Thy neighbour with disdain or haughtiness;
But with meek courtly grace
To weaker men give place;
Let the rabble crowd and throng, *thy* claims forbear
to press.

Be not like low-born boor,
Beguiled by the vile lure
Of sensuous appetite, who shoves aside,
Rudely, as the brute beast,
His fellow from the feast;
Till thy allotted turn in calm composure bide.

So shalt thou be found fit
With god-like men to sit,
Glad, welcome guest in heaven's fair banquet-hall;
Thy lot, however base,
If with thy lowly place
Content; "Give this man room," hear the feast-master call.

But if, when at thy feet
Earth's delicate and sweet
Are laid, thou look aside and pass them by,
In kingly rule thou'lt share,
The imperial purple wear,
Associate with the powers supreme that reign on high.

My soul fires at the thought,
How cheaply were it bought
With utmost sacrifice this sovereign good !—
To taste the joy divine,
Drink the new heavenly wine,
Love's choicest vintage,—feed on pure ambrosial food !

EPILOGUE.

Or ere I was aware,
My soul had caught an air
Breathed from no portico of Stoic rule;
The thoughts within me mount
Sprang from no classic fount,
Nor inspiration drew from philosophic school.

He felt not suffering
A mere indifferent thing,
Who groaned in spirit at the loved one's grave,
And, with sad cries and tears,
From that which man most fears
Thrice with strong agony his Father prayed to save.

His were the sympathies,
The susceptivities
With which each unsophisticate nature glows;
The fine sensitiveness,
Fruit of true nobleness,
To pain's keen fire-barbed darts doth the bared breast expose.

Reproaches broke his heart,
He felt the sword-like smart,
The coward disciples' flight, the traitor's kiss;
No arrow from the bow
Of sin-embittered woe
The Man-of-Sorrows' heart—their target true—could miss.

He crieth :—Learn of me,
Ye who go heavily,
Burdened and bowed beneath life's load of care :
The lowly one and meek
Bids the sad souls who seek
Contentment and true rest, His cross and passion share,—

Assured that loss and pain
Are fraught with lasting gain,
That, through the grave and darkling gate of death,
The spirit's parting strife,
We pass to fuller life,
Drink in immortal air as fails the mortal breath.

No dulling opiate, He,
Nailed to the accursèd tree,
Deigned to accept, his feelings to benumb;
To the last dregs would drain
The cup of mortal pain,
To its lowest depths the sea of human grief would plumb.

In no stern austere mood
Of haughty fortitude,
He bore the cruel cross, despised its shame;
Some strange, deep, secret joy
Availed his soul to upbuoy,
Through whose supporting power all evil he o'ercame,—

The joy that underlies
Pain, loss and sacrifice,
The peaceful, soul-reviving streams upmount
From the pierced, stricken heart,
Sore rent, and torn apart,
Till from its depths upsprings life's renovating fount.

And he who followed Christ
Nearest, and kept his tryst
Most true, all knowledge he had gained of yore
At learned Gamaliel's feet,
Forsook, ardent to greet
Truth's newly-risen sun, its splendours to explore.

In the lore initiate
Of Christ, he learned to rate
Aright the things of sense, life's brief hour lent;
The secret he has found,—
" To be abased, to abound,
In whatsoe'er state befell therewith to be content."

Yet even this wisdom pales
Before the light that hails
His dazzled vision, when, upon the cross,
In deep profound amaze,
Is fixed his steadfast gaze,
And prostrate there he learns his gains to reckon loss;

Desires henceforth but this,
Prays for no other bliss
Than absolute, complete conformity
To Him who suffered there,
Asks but that he may share
His lot who bled for him on that vile shameful tree.

Farewell, thrice- honoured sage !
Tho' from thine austere page,
Patience and fortitude my soul hath won,—
This light from Calvary
Dims thy philosophy,
Pales thy faint glow-worm light before the glorious
sun !

www.ingramcontent.com/pod-product-compliance
Lightning Source LLC
Chambersburg PA
CBHW020912230426
43666CB00008B/1417